Facebook for Business: A How-To Guide

ISBN: 1-4565-3896-9
ISBN-13: 9781456538965

Facebook for Business: A How-To Guide

Kaila Strong

VERTICAL MEASURES

Edited by: Ardala Evans
Cover design or artwork by: David Gould
Editorial coordination by: Elise Redlin-Cook

2011

Table of Contents

Introduction

With over 500,000,000 users on Facebook, 50% of which log in daily, Facebook is one of the most popular sites on the Internet. Facebook also presents itself as one of the fastest growing marketing opportunities for brands of all sizes. In this eBook we intend to enlighten readers of the true marketing opportunities offered on this ever popular social media platform.

Our experience stems from years of developing and implementing social media marketing campaigns focused on the social media giant. From eCommerce clients to B2B, our team has had the chance to work with a wide array of clientele. In this eBook we will share some of our experiences, and showcase our recommendations for managing Facebook profiles as an online marketing tool.

Yes, at times Facebook marketing can be difficult, but with this handy guide we hope to dispel the myths, inform, and explain in an easy to read format. We will cover what and how businesses can gain from Facebook including messaging, promotion, and measuring results. In addition, we'll give you details on customizing your Business Profile, the difference between Business Profiles and Groups, and how to effectively utilize all aspects of Facebook for your brand's benefit.

In February of 2011 Facebook implemented significant changes to business Pages. Not only were these changes instrumental in defining the future of Facebook, but in addition were extremely important to brands. This eBook has been updated to include pertinent information that will assist in developing the right Facebook campaign for any brand.

Section 1
Facebook

What is Facebook?

2003

In October of 2003, Harvard University student Mark Zuckerberg developed Facemash, described as Harvard's version of Hot or Not according to the Harvard Crimson. Zuckerberg's initial project utilized private dormitory ID images, which he obtained from protected areas of Harvard's computer network. While charges were dropped for his actions, Zuckerberg at one time faced expulsion for the breach of security, violation of copyrights, and violations of individual privacy.

2004

After the issues with Facemash, Zuckerberg developed "Thefacebook" and launched the site on February 4, 2004. The site was initially available to only students at Harvard, with the overall goal of allowing users to type in someone's name and be presented with a lot of information about them. Within a short time half the undergraduate students at Harvard were registered, and in March of 2004 Eduardo Saverin, Dustin Moskovitz, Andrew McCollum, and Chris Hughes joined the project to help promote "Thefacebook." Students at Stanford, Columbia, and Yale soon were given access to the site, and later to all Ivy League schools, NYU and MIT. With the success of the site, Zuckerberg and Moskovitz decided to drop out of school to pursue their new venture, and around that time the site was officially renamed Facebook.

2005

December of 2005 marked a huge milestone for Facebook: more than 5.5 million active users across 800+ college networks. This annual growth from 2004 to 2005 can be primarily attributed to the addition of photos for profile users, expansion to add high school networks, the addition of groups, and of course the acquisition of venture capital funds which allowed these changes to take place.

2006

By September of 2006, everyone age 13 and older was given access to Facebook, and work networks were added to the site linking together networks of coworkers across the globe. Since then, the site has seen unprecedented growth. From 2005 to 2006, active users rose from 5.5 million to 12 million. Investors such as Microsoft, Accel Partners, Greylock Partners and Paypal's co-founder Peter Thiel hopped on the social media bandwagon early, attributing to the growth. With increased venture capital funds, Facebook expanded into the mobile market, adding the Facebook Mobile feature which allowed users to access the social networking site on their mobile devices.

2007

International success of Facebook was evident in 2007, with over 2 million active Canadian users and 1 million users active in the United Kingdom. However, from a revenue generating standpoint, Facebook was still struggling; that is until Facebook advertising was launched. Working off of a pay-per-click model similar to other online advertising, the addition of Facebook Ads began generating a revenue stream for the site.

In November of 2007, Business Pages were introduced to allow brands, celebrities, and others to interact with their "fans" on Facebook.

2008

Users everywhere rejoiced when Facebook Connect became readily available, allowing users to share their information with third party websites and applications. Facebook Connect allows users to easily sign into third party sites via trusted authentication, and giving users dynamic use of third party sites. Other milestones in 2008 for Facebook were reaching 100 million active users, advanced privacy controls were launched and additional language translation applications for international user were added.

2009

Early in 2009, Facebook reached 150 million active users, and by December that number rose to 350 million active users. The "Like" feature was added in February of 2009, which some may say had a large role in increasing the number of active users. By giving users an ability to easily, with the click of a button, show their approval of basically anything shared on the site, Facebook catapulted usability and transitioned into the future of data collection across the web.

Facebook Today

Critics were pessimistic about the site's future earning potential as a free portal, only supported by advertising revenue. In late 2009, Facebook announced that for the first time in their existence the site turned a profit. With over 500 million active users, Facebook is continually developing and expanding. Now with Facebook Places and Facebook Questions, the social media platform is rivaling niche sites like LinkedIn, Google Places, Foursquare and others.

The controversy surrounding Zuckerberg and the Facebook brand has not stopped after charges were dropped by Harvard University. In 2004, ConnectU.com sued Zuckerberg, alleging he used their source code to develop his own site after committing to work for ConnectU.com. In 2009 Tyler and Cameron Winklevoss (and other parties) in connection with the ConnectU.com suit were awarded an estimated $65 million settlement, as leaked by the attorneys presiding over the case. In September of 2010, the issue was rehashed in the media, and in a legal battle, with the plaintiffs Tyler and Cameron Winklevoss alleging that the terms of the settlement have not been met, and that the agreed upon evaluation of Facebook's value was not correct.

Over the years many individuals and companies have attempted to sue the social networking site, citing a variety of reasons such as: privacy infringement, allowing defamous pages/groups, violation of intellectual properties, control of users content, and even for causing violent behavior.

Not to be outdone by the real-life legal battles, Hollywood premiered "The Social Network" in 2010, a reportedly fictional depiction of the Facebook legacy. The screenplay adapted by Aaron Sorkin, was based off the nonfiction book "The Accidental Billionaires," without involvement from Facebook staff. The movie has been well received by the public, changing many users' personal opinions about founder Mark Zuckerberg. Zuckerberg has spoken out about the inaccuracies portrayed in the movie, and friends have come to his defense as well.

It's evident that throughout the years Facebook, and the staff that runs the site, have gone through trials and tribulations. The fact remains, however, that the public has been extremely accepting and continuous in their support of using the website. Further growth and innovation is sure to come, with such strong minds steering the future of the social networking giant that is Facebook.

What Businesses Can Gain From Facebook

While Facebook was initially developed with the personal user in mind, over-time it was evident that businesses should have a place on Facebook as well, and not just through ads. As a business, celebrity, blog, non-profit group, city/state, inanimate object, or even just a silly idea, all are able to connect with users in a completely different way than through the use of a personal profile. How? With Facebook Pages.

Connecting with your fans on Facebook can make or break a brand's success online. With over half a billion users on the social networking platform, brands of any kind have an opportunity to market to prospects like never before. Facebook boasts that over 250 million users log into their accounts on a daily basis. Very few sites on the Internet can compete with those statistics.

For some, it's hard to understand just how their particular brand, product, or identity can successfully utilize Facebook. In some instances this stems from the lack of knowledge about how their audience utilizes the social media platform. Why would a user log in every day, participate, and interact? That can't possibly be your demographic. In most cases, however, it is.

From 12 year olds to 70 year olds, professionals to housewives, the spectrum of users on Facebook is varied. iStrategyLabs debuted their Facebook statistics report in January of 2010[1], showcasing the mean age and gender of the average US user. Surprisingly the average age of a US Facebook user is 35-54. The social media platform is no longer just a medium for high school students and college students to upload photos and share their status messages. It's a platform for business professionals, Baby Boomers and the like to reunite with past friends, colleagues, family members and even brands.

Facebook reports that the average user is connected to at least 80 community Pages, groups and events. Not only that, but users are sharing information too. More than 30 billion pieces of content such as links, images, posts, and notes are shared each and every month on Facebook. Users aren't just connected; they're engaged and willing to share your message. An October 2010 survey conducted by DDB shared some interesting data they gathered by questioning fans across six different countries[2]. Most of those surveyed, 41%, "Like" a Page because they want to take advantage of promotional benefits. 39% do so because they like the brand. 36% of respondents said when they "Like" a Page they intend on purchasing that brand's products more often than other brands.

As you can see from the numbers reported by not only Facebook, but third parties as well, the social networking giant can be an optimal place to get your brand and messaging noticed by new prospects. For your business, advertising is available on a pay-per-click basis (See Section 4 for more information.) Also available are Facebook Pages. On these fully interactive Pages, Administrators of Pages are able to engage with users who "Like" your business, blog, product or service. In future chapters we'll discuss how to properly engage with your fans, what types of messaging strategies are effective, and how to measure results.

SEO

Search engine optimization has morphed from years past to include social media activities in present campaigns. Social "signals" are currently studied by Google[3]. Does this mean social media efforts are a guaranteed way to optimize for search? No. Does this mean social media "signals" should be completely avoided? No.

Social "signals", while not ranking factors, can help in "discovery, trust concepts, temporal (velocity), context (semantics) and behavioral"[4]. Social does play a significant role in SEO and should be integrated for a well rounded campaign.

Link Building

While links from social networking sites, such as Facebook, are given a no-follow attribute, search engines ultimately still utilize links built on social networking sites in their algorithms as a "signal", discussed above. A video, link, or image that is shared hundreds of times on Facebook can provide benefits important to increasing awareness about your brand or your piece of content. It's only logical that search engines, if privy to this information, will use it as they see fit.

If you've checked Google Webmaster Tools lately you've likely seen Facebook backlinks showing up. Using Facebook to build authoritative backlinks can not only help diversify your backlink profile but also work towards building targeted traffic back to your site and your Facebook Page. Tagging other Pages in status updates assists in building targeted traffic and value for your site or Page.

For example, if your brand has written a blog post or piece of content on your site which features another brand, music artist, news station, etc…tag them in your Facebook status message by inserting an "@" symbol and their brand name (only available if you "Like" their Facebook Page). A drop down will appear and you'll need to click on the appropriate Page to tag the account. Don't forget to include a link to the piece of content residing on your site. The tagged message will show on their Page with a link back to your Facebook Page and a link to your piece of content. This is one way of adding value to your Facebook messaging strategy while also building additional backlinks to your content.

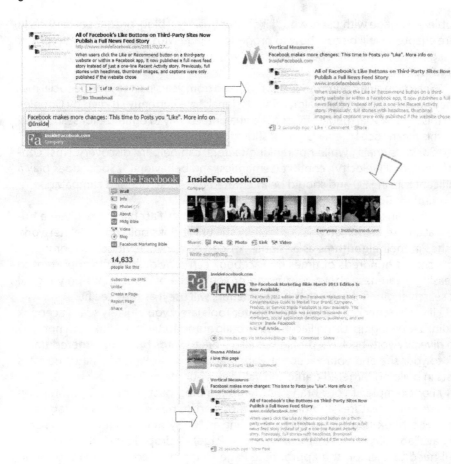

Popularity of content on social networking sites can work to your advantage as a business owner to positively impact your search engine rankings by diversifying the "signals" search engines use to help them to discover content, trust sources, determine what content is popular, semantic/keyword indicators and behavioral signals.

Online Reputation Management

"Owning" the first page of search results for your brand name is extremely important. Why? In some cases it's important to protect yourself from potential online reputation management nightmares in the future. For example, unexpectedly your company is sited in a rip off report online or a complaint with the BBB. If these types of results show up on the first page of search results for your brand name they could potentially deter others from doing business with you. By securing a variety of online profiles with your brand name, including social media profiles and other online properties, you stand a chance to push down negative brand results on search results pages should they pop up in the future.

Sales

Many forget that in the end improving your bottom line is the whole point of using social media marketing. If you aren't making money, and/or you aren't preventing loss of revenue then what's the point? Utilizing your Facebook profile to sell products, sell your services, or brand your company to earn more profit can be done.

eCommerce websites can often sell products easily on Facebook. Take, for example, a jewelry website who has built up a large fan base on Facebook. With regular messaging, coupons, specials, engagement, and even customized applications to help users browse jewelry selections, large sales can be made by directly interacting with prospects.

Fans might have questions before they buy, especially if you sell a product like jewelry which can be expensive and not an impulse buy for most. By answering questions quickly, offering alternative products, and using this opportunity to up sell you're sure to help and not hinder sales.

Your business and brand has a lot to gain from using Facebook. In future chapters we'll discuss proper ways to develop an overall strategy for your Facebook profile, how best to engage with prospects, and the ins-and-outs of profile design.

Personal Profile or Business Page: What's The Difference?

Your brand and business on Facebook have a few options to help connect you with users. Some choose to utilize Facebook Groups and others choose Business Pages. And others still use Facebook profiles. What's the difference?

Official Pages

Facebook developed Official Pages for businesses when they realized users were trying to connect and interact with brands, celebrities, or businesses in a way that the infant Facebook platform didn't support. Originally, businesses were using personal profile Pages and engaging with fans as friends. The problem arises, however, that a business doesn't have friends, they have users who "Like" them.

After the implementation of Facebook Official Pages, Facebook restricted businesses from having personal profile Pages. Please note: It's highly recommended that your business utilize Official Pages and not personal profile Pages. If you are currently utilizing a personal profile Page as a business Page, you're in jeopardy of violating Facebook's guidelines[5] and losing access to your account.

The February 2011 Facebook update to Pages allow businesses and brands to connect with fans on a more personal level. Administrators have the option to interact on Facebook as the Page. Administrators can switch back and forth between their own personal profiles and interacting on Facebook as the Page. This instrumental change made by Facebook now allows Pages to interact across the platform in many different ways. Comment on another profile as your branded Page, "Like" other pages as your branded Page and more. There are no longer "advantages" to have a personal profile Page instead of a branded Page.

Pages are the proper outlet for local businesses, brands, products, organizations, artists, bands or public figures. Official Pages often represent authentic brands, celebrities, or businesses and are administered by the verified appropriate official parties. Only verified parties are able to create Pages, interact with fans as the brand, celebrity or business and gain access to the statistics of Page activity and existing fan demographics.

Pages must be associated with an authentic personal profile, therefore, it's recommended that brands first set up an **authentic personal profile** for a user or users who will administer the Official Page for a brand and thereafter set up the Official Page. Don't worry; Administrators won't be publically associated with an Official Page. There are optional settings, however, that will show featured Administrators if your brand chooses to do so. Click "Edit Page" at the right of your Page. In the Administrators Dashboard click "Featured" and you're able to add featured Page owners/Administrators. By default none will be chosen and shared with your Fans.

Business Page or Group: Which is Right for Your Brand?

Facebook Groups are different than Pages. Groups are an extension of your personal actions. As an Administrator of a group your messages are attached to your personal profile, and your interactions are an extension of your profile. Groups offermore controls over participation and access can be restricted according to your needs. In some ways Groups are like a private chat stream where users can interact, but only certain users are allowed to interact depending on the Administrators' permissions.

Groups often revolve around a cause, issue, or activity and allow members to express their opinion, post content and discuss. Administrators can opt to have the group public or private and by invitation only. Administrators monitor and interact on a personal level, whereas Page Administrators interact as the brand.

A particular brand, movie, celebrity or business should determine their overall needs before deciding on a Group or Page. The chart below should help you determine which is best for your particular needs.

Interaction around a cause	Group
Interact as a brand with fans	Page
Disconnect from a personal account	Page
Connected from a personal account	Group or Page
Expect to exceed 5,000 fans/members	Page
Customize with applications	Page
Access to statistics	Page
Individual permission controls for fans/members	Group
Hosting an active discussion	Group or Page

Your business Page or Group should be built only by the appropriate business owner, or authorized personnel responsible for branding or messaging. As an Administrator you are responsible for all messaging, monitoring, branding, setting permission levels and notification settings. It's imperative to understand the impact of your actions on your branded Page or Group and instruct Administrators appropriately to maintain particular privacy or legal obligations important to your corporate brand or identity. For more information regarding Facebook's terms, it's recommended that you and your staff read the "Statement of Rights and Responsibilities" on Facebook.com.

Updates and Changes to Facebook Pages and Groups

Fans interacting with your Page or Group, by default, are allowed to write or post content on the Page or Group's wall, upload photos, upload videos, comment on photos, comment on videos, post links and see posts by "Everyone". Because anyone can become a fan it's recommended that Administrators monitor fan's activities and reduce permission settings for fans as applicable. With the new Facebook Page update, Administrators have increased notification settings. When someone "Like"s a Page, comments, uploads photos, etc…an e-mail can be sent to administators. Choosing email settings is easy: simply set your settings after clicking "Edit Page" on the top right of your Page. Once in the Administrators Dashboard section click "Your Settings" to manage email settings. Click "View all email settings for your Pages" to pick and choose which actionable items you'd like to be notified of for your Page.

Spamming, maliciousness, and inappropriate behavior can ruin a brand's Page if not monitored regularly. That's why it's important to regularly monitor your brand's Page or Group, usually on a daily basis. When members or fans post inappropriate messages, Administrators have the ability to flag the user as malicious and can even block the user from posting any further messages. After a short time as an Administrator you'll realize whether or not you want fans to have the ability to post messages to the wall, leave comments on photos, comments on videos and post links. Each area where users can interact will require constant monitoring and it's recommended that Administrators understand the pros and cons of allowing users to post user generated content on all aspects of a business's Page.

In October of 2010, Facebook announced changes to Groups. Personal profile users are able to "Group" friends together and share information with only that select group. Over time, Facebook has found that the average personal profile user requires more privacy and that their status updates deserve to be restricted to certain friends or "Groups." Personal profile users are now able to share data and information with just a select "Group" of friends.

Each of the updates made to Facebook in the past year are important in understanding which option is right for your brand. This eBook examines in more detail how to use Pages, as they are the preferred method for brands looking to engage on Facebook.

Instructions: How to Build Your Business Page Right

Now that you're sure your brand would be best represented by an Official Facebook Page let's discuss building it right.

The first step is to sign into your personal profile on Facebook.com that will act as the Administrator of your Page and next create a Page: http://www.facebook.com/pages/create.php. Six options are available: Create a local business or place, a company, organization or institution, a brand or product, an artist, band or public figure, entertainment, or cause or topic. Choose the right option for your brand:

- Local Business or Place: Several options are available, and geared mostly to local brick-and-mortar locations such as automotive dealers, bars and clubs, grocery stores, hotels, restaurants, etc…
- Company, Organization or Institution: Many options, more specific than those listed above including designations such as consumer products, professional services, retail, websites, etc…
- Brand or Product: Specific categories are available under this option. Clothing, electronic distributor, pet supplies, or software provider? Choose this option.
- Artist, Band or Public Figure: A limited number of available options with this type of page, but includes public figure, athlete, actor, model, sports team and even writer.
- Entertainment: Concert venue, Magazine, Radio Station, or TV show? Choose this option.
- Cause or Topic: Somewhat self explanatory, this Page is an applicable choice if your brand revolves around a non-profit cause or interesting/funny/pop culture topic.

Make sure to enter the correct Page name after choosing which type of page. If your primary goal of establishing an Official Page is for branding, it's best to stick to the name you're known as.

Finally, agree to the official rules (be sure to review the Facebook terms so you know what you're getting yourself into http://www.facebook.com/pages/create.php#!/terms.php), and click "Get Started."

Once you've clicked "Get Started" you'll be directed to your new and improved Facebook Page. If you haven't at this point reviewed the Facebook terms (http://www.facebook.com/pages/create.php#!/terms.php)—do it.

The next step is to start filling out your profile with all the needed information to complete your profile. Facebook does a great job of detailing the items they suggest you fill in to complete your fan page, they are as follows:

1) Add an image, which will be used as the basic image your page will be known for. A few tips: Make a customized image, using every pixel of the 180 x 540 pixels allowed. When designing an image try to place your pictoral mark or logo at the top of the image. Facebook will create a thumbnail of your profile image to show on your wall alongside any status message updates. The thumbnail is square, so keep this in mind when designing a rectangular image. In order to change the thumbnail of your photo click "Edit Page" on the right of your Page and click "Profile Picture" in the Administrators Dashboard. Under your image you'll need to click

"Edit Thumbnail". Drag the image to adjust to the proper section you'd like shown as the thumbnail, which appears next to each of your status message updates. This may require editing the image you already uploaded as your picture so as not to crop any of your logo out of view on the thumbnail.

2) If you have been judicious about staying in contact with prior customers and friends of your brand, then step 2 will benefit you. Tell your personal friends about your Page and import your contacts via a contact file (usually exported from the CRM or system you're currently utilizing). Another option is given to sign into your e-mail where your contacts reside (such as Gmail, Yahoo, Hotmail, etc...). A maximum of 5,000 is set on the number of contacts you can import. This step is extremely important when starting off your social media marketing campaign as you will want to connect with your existing clients and prospects. Also, give them a chance to recommend your brand to their personal friends. Continually import your contacts to connect in yet another way and further the impact of your brand in addition to traditional marketing efforts.

3) Provide some basic information for your profile. It's always best to fill in as much information as possible when building social profiles. Click "Edit Page" at the top right side of your Page. Click "Basic Information" and fill in as much as possible. If the category section isn't filled out correctly you can change it in the "Basic Information" section.

Any area where a potential keyword or link could be placed should be utilized (within reason of course.) Add general information about your business, your full website address, business address, operating hours, etc. It's always recommended that you provide descriptions and information that is unique from the standard copy on your website. Don't copy and paste information direct from your website, but rather make it unique and specific for your Facebook audience.

Take this time to also set permissions by clicking "Manage Permissions" and "Your Settings". Each setting and permission is very self explanatory. It's important to have forethought in determining which settings and permissions to choose. For a brand like an educator monitored by an accreditation committee or a publically traded company monitored by the FDIC, we recommend limiting the activities of fans. Uncheck boxes such as "Users can write or post content on the wall", "Users can add photos" or "Users can add videos" located in the "Manage Permissions" section. Brands less concerned can increase notification settings located in the "Your Settings" section to monitor when users do write or post content on the wall, add photos or add videos. This will still give you the necessary tools needed to monitor fan activities the moment it happens. Prior to the February 2011 changes with Facebook Pages, Administrators weren't given the option to receive Pages notifications via e-mail which made it a laborious to monitor fan activities on a daily basis.

4) Next, start posting status updates to your Wall. A Facebook status message update is limited to 420 characters, including spaces. In Section 3 we'll examine how to target your message, examples of successful status message updates for your Business Pages and the rules of engagement with fans.

Click "Share" to post your first update. A status message update can consist of words, links to third party sites, events, video, or pictures by clicking the icons shown above the status message box that asks "What's on your mind?" when you are using Facebook as your Page.

Page Administrators can also customize who will see status message updates by clicking the lock shown in the status message box (after a message has been typed). Choose "Customize" from the drop down menu items that appear when you click on the lock. Customizing your message to be shown to fans in a specific location, or to fans who don't speak English, allows Page Administrators to cater messaging to specific demographics.

At any time you can delete status message updates posted to your wall by clicking the "X" (shown when you hover over an already posted status message on a page you are the admin of). Try posting a test message and delete it so you can see how this step works.

Try tagging others in your status updates, which can be done by adding an "@" symbol in a status message. Start typing a Page's name after an "@" symbol and select which Page you'd like to tag in your message. With Facebook's update made in February of 2011 you're able to interact on your page as your brand. Simply go to your Page and click "Use Facebook as 'Your Page'" an option located at the right of your Page. Use the search function of Facebook to find other Pages to interact on third party Pages as your brand, including Pages you'd like to tag in messages. Think about the cross messaging capabilities of tagging or connecting with other Pages—capitalize on the fans built by a similar brand, a brand that is a partner with your company, or a brand that has a similar demographic to your own.

5) Promote your page on your website with a Like Box. Click the "Add Like Box" button (Step 5 under "Get Started" or click "Marketing" in the Administrators section of your Facebook Page, and customize your own Like Box. Customize the width, color scheme and other specifics. Click "Get Code" and give to your webmaster to add to your brand's website. There are other ways to promote your new Facebook Business Page as well: announcing your new page in weekly/daily/monthly newsletters, suggest your page to your existing friends of your personal Facebook profile, add a Facebook icon to your blog or website, or add a "Like" button throughout your website (go to http://www.facebook.com/pages/create. php#!/terms.php for more information). Promoting your Business Page will help you gain momentum in building up a fan base on Facebook.

6) The final step in setting up your Facebook Business Page is to connect your page with your mobile device, if you have one. By connecting your mobile phone to Facebook you have the option of sending mobile email to upload photos or post status updates, or send mobile text messages to post status updates.

7) Last steps: Once your Page is setup, it's recommended that you become familiar with the Administrators Dashboard of your Page, which we've discussed previously. Click the "Edit Profile" button, located on the right side of your Page, to be taken to the Administrator's Dashboard.

The Administrator's Dashboard allows Administrators to manage settings, permissions, basic information for your Page, edit the profile picture, feature other Pages or even the Administrator's personal profiles of your brands Page, promote (see Section 4 for more information), manage other Administrators, view applications (discussed more in this section), edit mobile settings, view insights (see Section 5 for more information), and get help with your questions.

The above steps are just the beginning to setting up your Business Page. There are a number of customization options to make your page different from the rest. From customized applications to landing pages for non-fans, there are many options for your Business Page.

Customization Options

A standard Facebook page has 8 left side bar or "Tab" options, such as "Wall", "Info", "Photos", "Discussions" and "Reviews". Clicking on the "Edit Page" button and clicking "Applications" will show the Administrator any other left side bar options available. For fans, simply clicking the "More" button on the left hand side of the Page will show options that aren't currently being displayed. As an Administrator, you have the ability to choose which options should be displayed and viewed, additional items to add and further customization.

By clicking "More" there will be additional options presented which include "Less" and "Edit". By clicking "Edit" as the Administrator you're able to click and drag side bar options to their desired locations. For example, if you wish to edit the first six options presented to a Fan on a business Page simply click "Edit" after clicking the "More" button and click and drag the desired option to its proper place. Wall— The area on a Business Page or Profile that allows fans to see your status message updates, post their own messages, and see other fans messages as well. The default setting for the "Wall" is to show posts by "Everyone". Facebook will automatically customize these messages to show status message updates that are most relevant to a particular user. Status messages that receive a large amount of "Like"s or comments will be located near the top of a brands "Wall".

Attachments can be posted on the wall including: video, links, events and more. To limit the posting abilities for fans, an Administrator must "Manage Permissions" in the "Edit Page" section of a Page.

Info—A section on a Business Page or Profile which gives details and information about a brand or person. Details such as preferences, address, phone number, web address, general information, etc. This information is editable after clicking "Edit Page" on the right side of a Page.

Photos—A section on a Business Page or Profile which allows a brand or person to upload photos, organize photos in albums and add captions to albums. Photos on the new Facebook Pages randomly show at the top of a Page. Five photos are represented, normally in random order. This new change to Facebook Pages emphasizes the need for Pages to have relevant and interesting photos displayed at all times. Fans can even upload photos, which are organized in one album in the

Photos tab. Many brands are encouraged to have fans upload photos. This user generated content can help catapult a brand into the mainstream.

Discussions—A section on a Business Page which allows brands to post questions or items that are discussion worthy, requiring more interaction than those on a normal status update. Fans then reply to these items. The discussion section often acts as an engagement platform for fans to get questions answered and can be a customer service portal as well.

Reviews—A section on a Business Page which allows fans to rate a particular brand and their services. Administrators cannot delete reviews however bad or good they are.

Links—A section on a Business Page or Profile which aggregates all the links that have been added to a brand or person's Wall.

Notes—A section on a Business Page or Profile, much like a blog. Customize notes specific to your Page or Profile's audience, tag other users or brands, and embed photos. Users can also import their own blog to auto post status message updates when a new blog post goes live. Simply import a RSS feed by editing import setting in the Notes tab. Notes are a great way to say what your brand wants to say when you need more than the 420 character limit of a status message update.

Video—A section on a Business Page or Profile which aggregates all the videos uploaded to a Page or Profile.

Events—A section on a Business Page or Profile which aggregates all the events your Page or Profile has hosted. Events can be created for many things such as attending your store's sale, participating in an online contest, attending an open house and more.

Applications

There are thousands of applications for your Facebook Business Page. Applications are premade add-ons for your Facebook Page or Profile, which require very little technical knowledge and are essentially ready for use with a few clicks of a button. To search for available applications that don't come standard on your Business Page, simply put your search query in the Search box at the top of the Facebook platform and click the magnifying glass to submit your search query. Another option is to first click "Edit Page" and go to "Apps". At the bottom of the "Apps" section click "Browse more applications" to view additional applications for your Page.

The set of applications below are viewed by Mashable and social media experts as the essential applications for your Business Page. Depending on your particular brand's needs, each of the applications offer something different to customize your Business Page.

Static FBML—This application adds versatility every Business Page or Profile needs in an easy to use section or series of sections. Insert CSS, HTML code or FMBL code (Facebook Markup Language) and customize the static FBML box on your Page. Simply add the app to your Page by clicking "Add to my page" after searching for this application as instructed above.

Edit the application from the Administrator Dashboard. First click "Apps" from the dashboard. Locate the FBML box application and click "Go To Application" to customize the title of the section and to enter in your HTML or FBML code. Multiple FBML boxes can be added as sections to your Page, simply click "Add another FBML box" to do so. Facebook has a limit of 520 pixel widith for any custom section. Keep this in mind for images and tables added using HTML or FBML code.

As of March 11, 2011 Facebook will no longer allow Static FBML boxes. Existing Static FBML boxes will continue to work, however. iFrames are the preferred method to develop customized "Tabs" on Facebook. iFrames allow for increased usability and flexibility, integrating analytics information, utilizing standard HTML/CSS/Javascript just like any other web page does. Prior to February 10, 2011, Facebook did not allow iFrames on "Tabs". iFrames require a more technical knowledge of web applications, Facebook Software Development Kits (SDKs) and XFBML tags. While Static FBML boxes did allow even novices to venture into the world of Facebook "Tab" customization, this new roll out by Facebook reduces that ability. At the time this eBook was written, several developers have provided tutorials which give an in depth examination of iFrames and how they relate to Facebook customization. In the future we expect more publications to be made available which will detail Facebook customization in depth.

iFrames—This application allows you to embed an externally held Web page in a "Tab". iFrames are not hosted within Facebook and can use JavaScript, standard HTML, and standard HTML. Developers must be familiar with Facebook Software Development Kits (SDKs) and XFBML tags, in addition to a Web-accessible server in order to upload files needed to customize your "Tab". A great tutorial has been developed by Hyperarts.com, and can be found in a recent blog post.[6]

FBML to iFrame—A free application by Wildfire, developed after Facebook's announcement about Static FBML Apps, is free for a limited time. This application will convert Static FBML "Tab"s to iFrames. The application can be found on their website, or: iframes.wildfireapp.com. This application allows businesses to easily develop their own customized "Tab" in addition to using "attractive image and HTML based landing pages".

Social RSS—This application imports your blog RSS feed and publishes to your wall, in addition to aggregating previous posts into one easy to read section. Social RSS allows you to customize how a post is posted to your Page and how a link to the post would be added to your Page. Even an auto-"Like" function is available to allow for an auto-"Like" on each of the posts you share. Importing your blog to Facebook helps increase the reach of your message, gives fans the opportunity to interact with your brand, and links back to your blog to help increase site traffic. As discussed earlier, importing your blog also allows for increasing backlinks to your blog, important in increasing the authority of your backlink profile.

Involver Free Applications (Involver.com)—The premiere Facebook application developer, offers Business Page owners the ability to set up a free account and add 2 free applications to their Page. You can choose from a RSS feed customized section much like Social RSS, a Twitter aggregator, YouTube Channel aggregator, Flickr application, PDF application and many others. Simply set up an account and follow the instructions to setup and add the applications to your Business Page after exploring Involver.com's website. Involver's applications are powerful tools to help you engage with fans and offer customization options for any Business Page. They offer a paid option which can be helpful for a large business in need of vast customization options.

Manage Permissions—A final customization option for Page Administrators is to manage permissions. Set your page's visibility after clicking "Edit Page" and viewing the "Manage Permissions" section of the Administrators section. Often Administers check particular boxes depending on their requirements for their business Page. The box titled "Only admins can see this Page" is checked only when your Page is under construction, or restricted to specific countries. If your site only caters to a specific country you may consider restricting specific countries by entering them into the section labeled "Country restrictions". If you offer services or products with age restrictions make sure to set this up accordingly under the section labeled "Age Restrictions". Also set wall spam filters and posting abilities for fans. If you find that your fans post malicious content regularly, set a restriction accordingly as well.

Additional Customization

After 25 "Like"s you're able to set a vanity URL for your Page. Not sure what a vanity URL is? A vanity URL is a customizable URL for your brand. Facebook allows your Page to reside on a URL of your choosing on the Facebook.com domain. Already have 25 "Like"s? Sign into Facebook and go to http://www.facebook.com/username to set up your own personalized URL. Make sure you are using Facebook as the personal user you've signed into Facebook as before going to Facebook.com/username. To set a Page vanity URL click the dropdown and click on your Page name. You'll be given an option, only once, to set a URL.

A vanity URL is an easy way for those familiar with your brand to find your Page, but also can have SEO benefits as well. Choose a URL that will be familiar to users who are interested in interacting with your brand. Some have opted to use keywords in their URL string. While this might appeal to some of you, remember: you can't change your URL—it's permanent! If you don't want a competitor or spammer to set your brand name as their own vanity URL and you want your Page easily found then we suggest you set your vanity URL as a your brand name from the start.

Tools for Management

After your Business Page has been set up, the maintenance period begins. Uploading content, posting status message updates, responding to comments, engaging with fans, it can all get a bit overwhelming. Many tools have been developed to help.

There are a wide variety of free and paid tools that help connect your social profiles and each offer their own set of pros and cons. Using the graphic below, choose which platform (listed across the top) that connects to the social profile s your brand is most active on. Utilizing a tool such as Hootsuite, Seesmic, or Tweet-deck to help manage cross platform activities allows you to post-date messages, easily reply to comments, send out the same message on multiple social profiles with the click of a button and monitor engagement through analytics (see Section 5 for more information).

Involver, the Facebook application developer mentioned previously, has developed a social media platform to help Administrators with Facebook and other sites. It seamlessly integrates with many social networks, and offers a variety of monitoring options to help you manage your social media marketing campaign.

As a brand, or even an agency managing your client's social media marketing, you have many options as far as cross platform branding tools go. Examining all of your options based on the social profiles that are important to you will help make the final decision of choosing one of the above tools we've highlighted.

Section 3
Messaging

With over 500,000,000 active users on Facebook, your brand has the opportunity to connect with and influence prospects. Fifty percent of these users log in daily, and it's up to Page Administrators to make sure a brand stands out above the 900,000,0000 objects that users interact with regularly (pages, groups, events, and community pages.)

Demographic Profiling

Understanding your audience is the first step in tailoring your messaging, and promoting your Page to stand out above the rest. Age bands, social class bands, and gender are components which make up demographic profiles. Analyzing how each thinks, interacts, and purchases online isn't an exact science, but can help you maximize your messaging when used and tested.

Statistics and studies for online social behavior are still young, when compared to demographic profiling of other advertising mediums such as radio and television. However, social behavior can be more closely examined and more factors taken into consideration due to the large data set and ease of access to that data. Use the steps below to help you determine where your audience is, and the process to target your message for the greatest impact.

Step 1: Social Technographic Profile

Forrester Research, an independent company specializing in research in business and technology, surveyed over 26,000 individuals to come up with their Social Technographic Profile[7]. Their data places online social users into seven different social participation sets. Depending on the age, gender and country of your demographic, you'll be presented with a "snapshot" of the online social behaviors of your audience. Taken with a grain of salt, the outcome of using this Social Technographic Profiling tool can help you understand your overall social audience, and how they participate online to help guide your messaging.

Step 2: Third Party Facebook Demographic Data

Web analyst Nick Gonzalez created CheckFacebook.com, a site which offers core data such as the total number of users, 10 largest countries and age distribution. Data from Quantcast shows more information for Facebook's active U.S. audience such as age, earnings per year, education level, race and sites the audience also likes. Use these sites with your social demographic in mind. Do they have a large voice on Facebook compared to other countries, races, education levels and earners?

Step 3: Facebook Demographic Data

Data from Facebook Advertising shows even further information about your demographic, straight from the source. Head on over to Facebook's advertising portal and create a sample ad. In Step 2 of creating an ad you can set your targets and see an "Estimated Reach" of your ad should you make it go live. We'll discuss more about how you can use Facebook advertising in Section 4, but for messaging and demographic research, utilize the advertising portal to understand potential reach for different audiences. You'll likely need to revisit this information within a few short months as Facebook is growing at monumental speed. Expect the data to change with the growth. Who are your targeted users? What are they interested in? What other brands are they fans of?

Step 4: More Third Party Data

With the increasing popularity of Facebook as a marketing channel comes data. HubSpot, a leader in inbound marketing software, always provides great data and most recently they've studied Facebook as an inbound marketing channel. Their analysis of data pulled direct from Facebook[8] has allowed them to profile Facebook activity by Age and determine how the number of friends, wall posts, interests listed, activities, etc…differs from age group to group. Where does your demographic fall into their graph[9]?

Step 5: Use What You've Learned

Demographic research certainly isn't a one-size-fits-all solution for every brand hoping to find success on Facebook, but with a bit of common sense you've likely gathered a lot of useful information. Where your demographic hangs out, what they're interested in, the brands that they are connected with, and the potential reach your brand might have. Keep this information in mind as you examine targeting your message to your audience.

Targeting Your Message

Trends in social media have morphed the way businesses advertise to consumers. Gone are the days of one-way communication, and here to stay are two-way engaged conversations with your target market. Learning techniques to engage the demographic you identified using the information in the previous pages is what you'll learn in the following few pages.

In part, targeting your message to your demographic will require trial and error. Continuous testing with particular messaging strategies, listed below, and measuring their success or failure will help you figure out the right strategy for the fans you build on your Page. Monitor each of the following when trying out targeted messaging strategies:

Number of "Likes" and When

Which types of messages produce more "Likes" and at what time of day? Data analyzed by HubSpot can provide you with some general information regarding time and day. They've found weekends are the best time to message because those messages are shared more often[10]. A study by Virtue discovered that the biggest spike in conversations on Facebook happens at 3PM EST[11]. They've also found that messages posted at the top of the hour tend to be more successful than at other times.

Shares per message

Using Facebook search you can get a good feel for how often your messages are shared by simply doing a search for a particular message sent out from your business Page.

At the end of February 2011 Facebook made yet another change to the site: previously when those who "Like" your business Page indicate that they "Like" a particular post on your wall or a particular page on your website (if you have the "Like" button installed) it would show on their personal profile in a simple one line format. It would also show in news feeds of friends but less prominently. Those who "Like" your business Page also had the option to "Share" an individual post from your wall and post it on their wall with their comments. Now, whether a comment is added or not, when a user indicates they "Like" a post on your wall or "Share" a post with friends it will show as a full feed on their own wall and will also show more prominently in the news feeds of their friends[12].

Insights per message

In Section 5 we'll discuss Facebook Insights, analytics available to each Page which keeps record of data such as "Like" count, limited demographic data, interaction per post and more. Use Facebook Insights to determine the success or failure of each individual message placed on your business Page's wall.

Targeted Messaging Examples

Q & A

Simply ask fans questions. What did you do this weekend? Would you rather watch: 10 hours of Lifetime Movie Network or be forced to watch grass grow for two days straight? What was the last check you wrote for? Do you often check your credit history? Each of these questions can help you figure out what fans do in their leisure time, their preferred method of punishment, their spending habits and their attention to spending. Noticing patterns in responses from fans, and figuring out what gets them to engage, can all help in targeting your messaging for the greatest impact.

Content

Sharing content with your fans is an effective way to gain success on Facebook. If you're seen as an expert in your industry, continually "sharing and caring," and sparking discussion, then one would assume that the next time one of your fans is in the market to purchase what you sell they'll come to you.

Facts

Everyone loves a bit of trivia. If you know trivia about something specific in your industry, share it. Examples like those on DidYouKnow.org are interesting and can get you noticed. Did you know that the muscle that lets your eye blink is the fastest muscle in your body? Did you know, if a soup is too salty, to add raw cut potatoes and discard them after cooking to get rid of the saltiness? Did you know you can take pictures of a mirage? These factoids are perfect for an eye doctor, cooking fanatic, and photographer looking to engage with their fans.

Statistics

Searching a keyword in your industry paired with the word "statistics" will show a plethora of stats that you can share with your fans. This is a simple way to engage and share.

Deals

Coupons, sweepstakes, giveaways, contests we all love winning something, especially if it's free. What better way to understand your customers than through a promotion? Gather data, analyze it and notice trends.

Humor

Some might not feel comfortable integrating humor into their messaging, but we all love a good laugh. There are thousands of humor/joke sites available on the web. Search them out, and find a few jokes for your industry to share with fans. Or heck, if you're funny enough, make up a few of your own.

Simplicity

Sometimes, simplicity is the best way to go about your Facebook messaging. Your fans might not want to engage daily (or even monthly), or you might work in an industry that doesn't support a lot of discussion (think hemorrhoid cream product.) That's when simple messaging, short and to the point, will have the greatest impact.

Use the information you gather when experimenting with any of the above targeted messaging techniques or unique ideas on your own. What works? What doesn't? Continue to target your messaging and find the right mix that: 1) engages your fans, 2) completes goals you set for your brand—whether traffic, conversions, mentions, rankings, fan increases, etc…and 3) creates brand advocates for your Page.

Rules of Engagement

Developing rules for your team responsible for messaging and branding on your business's behalf is extremely important to your future success. These rules can help limit miscommunication, branding mistakes, address issues as they happen, and offer the proper chain of communication when dealing with these issues. Some of your rules might include:

- Be transparent—always try to be as transparent as possible, put a face to your brand and connect with fans on a deeper level.
- Have a code of conduct—be as specific as possible about how you want those in charge of messaging on behalf of your brand to act. Set boundaries, rules and regulations.
- Don't talk at, talk with—it's a two-way conversation not a one-way conversation. Become a resource, confidant and expert to your fans in a given industry.

- Address gripes and complaints with clear focus—offer speedy resolutions to issues with products or services, try to address these items off the public forum and with clear focus.
- Customer service policies are a must—be as specific as possible about how you want customer service issues to be addressed, how often refunds or coupons should be given, who authorizes those decisions, when an issue should be elevated to upper management, etc...
- Acknowledge and thank brand advocates—have a policy to address and thank those that are brand advocates or evangelists: discounts, announcements, admiration, etc. Not every brand advocate deserves something free, but a shout-out can't hurt.
- Be consistent—both in your messaging on Facebook and across platforms. Often when multiple users are in charge of managing messaging some disconnect can happen. Be as specific as possible about your consistent messaging, a social media editorial calendar can help.
- Add value—ensure your messaging and actions add value to the Facebook community, helps others, sometimes before your self-interests are met.
- Be exciting—determine the qualities it takes to be exciting, be share worthy.
- Admit mistakes—they do happen, but aren't the end of the world. Establish guidelines to admitting mistakes, when to delete messages and how to address them.
- Avoid trolls—some will try to defame your brand, don't stoop to their level: rise above. Sometimes a simple delete and ban of a particular user is better than addressing their issues. Establish a plan of action.
- Don't give up—establish guidelines to avoid giving up on creating exciting messaging, monitoring and responding regularly.
- Have clear internal response time standards—establish how often your staff will monitor and respond to items on the Page. Have a checklist of items to check daily, weekly or monthly.
- Take your efforts elsewhere on Facebook—with the updates to Facebook Pages in February 2011 your brand can interact on other Pages as your Page. Confusing as it might sound, it's an easy concept. Click "Use Page as 'your brand name'" which is listed on the right of your Page. Then use Facebook search to find other pages that are similar to your own and start interacting with them. "Like" them and their stories will start to show on your own Page's newsfeed. Get in the habit of clicking "Use Page as 'your brand name'" and check the newsfeed to interact with other Pages on a regular basis.

Establishing your rules of engagement doesn't mean they're set in stone. Change it up and experiment as necessary. Don't be surprised if something comes up that you aren't prepared for. Deal with what comes along and use it as an example for the future.

Section 4

Promotion

Once you've built the perfect Facebook Page, then what? That's where promotion comes in. Think of your new Facebook Page like an extension of your website. Your website needs promotion and so does your Facebook Page. Just as there are many options for website marketing, there are several options for your Facebook Page which includes Facebook advertising and cross platform promotion.

Facebook Advertising and Cross Platform Promotion

In 2007 Facebook developed their advertising portal, opening up the door for many businesses to promote their websites online in a newly emerging and exciting way. Similar to Pay-Per-Click (PPC) and Cost-Per-Impression (CPI or CPM) advertising on search engines, Facebook advertising allows advertisers to develop a custom ad, target users, and pay for advertising per click and per impression. The key to a successful ad campaign, however, isn't as simple as you might think.

Facebook offers a Guide to Facebook Advertising[13], which offers great guidance on managing your budget, targeting the right audience, tracking performance, improving your ads and more. There are a few things to remember before getting started:

- Know what you want to accomplish: Is it fans you're looking for? Traffic? Brand recognition? Conversions?
- Figure out how much you want to spend. Testing out your ad campaigns with a limit of a $25 spend per day will allow you to track and test with minimal impact on your bottom line until you're more comfortable.
- Understand who your target demographic is. In Section 3 we suggested making a sample ad and testing out different features of Facebook Advertising. If you haven't done so already, check it out. The information might just surprise you and make you change your mind on who your ad should target. Be sure to target the messaging in your ad to your demographic[14], mindful of what we discussed in Section 3.
- Review Facebook's Advertising Guidelines[15], which includes restrictions such as: landing pages, when linking to third parties, cannot have pop-ups; ads must have limited references to "Facebook"; ads cannot reference such things as tobacco, scams, illegal activities, inflammatory religious content, etc; ads cannot contain or promote spam. Get familiar with the restrictions.

- Create your ad; you're limited to 135 characters of text and one photo. Design an ad, or use an existing logo, that is of high quality and similar to the content you're promoting. Use a landing page in your ad that goes to the page you're looking to promote. Depending on your goals this page can be: your website, a Facebook event, or, of course, your Facebook Page.
- Not quite sure Facebook advertising is right for you? Check out some of Facebook's success stories to inspire you[16].

Brands like Einstein's Bagels and Victoria's Secret have used Facebook advertising to help promote their Facebook Pages, giving extra incentive to become a fan by offering free coupons for bagels or underwear, respectively. When you come up with the right ad, your opportunities are endless.

When using Facebook's Marketplace ads your ad has the opportunity to show social endorsements within or around the ad, largely credited with the success of campaigns like Einstein's Bagels and Victoria's Secret. Social endorsements include showing your audience additional information such as friends of theirs who have interacted with your ad, page or event. This social value ad is something that other advertising platforms don't offer. Facebook also offers premium ads for those with very large budgets and have creative advertising plans in mind. It's suggested you contact their advertising team directly to discuss ads of this caliber.

Cross Platform Promotion

Promoting your Facebook Page throughout the web is yet another way to advertise; garnering the attention of those highly sought after fans. Simple as it might seem, the first place to start is your own website. Adding Facebook "Like" buttons to your website, social media icons on your homepage and in newsletters, Facebook sharing capabilities on your blog, and occasional promotions through your blog itself are ways you can utilize your website to promote your Page.

Don't forget about all of your other advertising as well! Big brands like Toyota, Choice Hotel, and others utilize their television ads to promote their Facebook Pages, YouTube channel, and Twitter accounts. Print ads can help promote your online social profiles as well. Add a Facebook logo to your mailers, print-offs in store, and even on your store receipts or invoices. Customers, vendors, window shoppers, television watchers, can all be Facebook fans too right?

Social Media Editorial Calendar

In Section 2 we discussed at length tools to help you manage your Facebook Page. Each of these tools can also be used for cross platform promotion. Manage your Twitter account, Facebook, MySpace, and LinkedIn with an easy to use program that helps reduce the management time it takes to monitor your social profiles. The important thing to remember is consistency of messaging, something we discussed in Section 3, but worth mentioning again. A likely answer to organize specific messaging—a social media editorial calendar.

Similar to an editorial calendar you might utilize for your blog, adding a social component does wonders to keep you organized. The below calendar is an example of a blog editorial calendar with a social spin. As you can see, the calendar utilizes:

- Specified days for different social media platform interaction
- Themes consistent throughout the month
- Clear and consistent messaging: ask questions every 1st Friday on Twitter and LinkedIn, post questions every 3rd Friday on Facebook, promote the blog on all social platforms on Monday's and Thursday's, etc.

A more in-depth editorial social calendar might include such items as:

- Specific messages to be placed on your social media platforms, pre-planned throughout the month and ready for scheduling (note: Hootsuite, Tweetdeck and Seesmic offer post-dating of Facebook Page status messages)
- Advertising campaigns
- Contests and promotions
- Coupons
- Days to provide reporting
- Strategy meetings to come up with the next months calendar

Applications

In Section 2 we explained how to customize your Facebook Page with applications such as those offered by Involver.com or by other developers. What we didn't discuss at that time was how you can also use applications to promote your own Facebook Page.

Anyone can develop a Facebook application with the right tools, creative idea, extensive knowledge of Facebook Markup Language (FBML), and knowledge of Facebook's Platform Policies[17]. Businesses too can develop applications, with their brand front and center of a potentially viral idea. From surveys and games to shopping applications and contests, the applications a brand can develop are many. The problem arises when trying to promote such application.

Promotion Guidelines

Facebook's Promotion Guidelines[18] are strict and quite rigorous. Spammers have caused Facebook to be on guard to prevent their users from malicious intent. As such, guidelines have been put in place to prevent even the most well intentioned business from true freedom. Get familiar with Promotion Guidelines if you intend to develop an application or undergo a custom contest or sweepstakes (discussed further in Section 4). Noteworthy restrictions include:

- Contests or promotions must be run through applications and are only allowed to have contestants enter on the canvas page of the application or on the Facebook page's application box.
- Specific disclosures must be added to all promotion applications you administer through the Facebook Platform.
- Photo contests can't require users to enter, and manually manipulate their profile photo.
- Entry to contests and promotions cannot require users to update their status message.
- Entry to contests and promotions cannot require users to become a fan.

Don't let the rules discourage you. Working with Facebook application developers such as Involver.com or even Wildfire.com can be cost effective and help to promote your Facebook Page as well.

Contests and Sweepstakes

The overall goal of a Facebook contest or sweepstake is to help promote your brand, encourage more fans to "Like" your Page, engage your users to share your page with their friends, and add variety to your messaging. While the rules we discussed in the previous pages might scare the average user, contests and sweepstakes when run correctly can offer a wide range of benefits for your brand.

Adidas, Dunkin Donuts, Papa Johns, IKEA, and many other big brands have all utilized contests and sweepstakes to promote their Facebook Pages. When done well it makes your fans happy. Many of these brands have stated they gained significant benefits from running these contests and sweepstakes.

Tips

- Follow the rules—The last thing you want to do is get your Page banned on Facebook. Follow the rules, get permission from Facebook before running any contest or sweepstake, and you'll avoid potential danger.
- Measure your results (see Section 5 for more information)
- Be creative—Thinking outside the box can turn an otherwise traditional promotion into something that has potential to become viral. Look online for inspiration: social bookmarking sites, your competitors, throughout Facebook and ask your employees. You can get inspiration from anywhere.

- Think about your demographic and potential partnerships—Some brands have found success in partnering with other businesses to give away some great prizes. Who is your demographic, and what other businesses can help you promote to your demographic? Try a partnership and join efforts for the greater good.
- Look for opportunities to leverage content in the future—If you're developing a contest, think about user generated content that contestants could provide you in order to enter: poems, pictures, videos, comments, these are all user generated content that can be your property and reused in future efforts (of course, if stated in the entry rules.)
- Leverage cross platform promotion—Don't just rely on word of mouth to spread the news about your contest. Use your other social media profiles, your print advertising, in store advertising, newsletters, etc. Coordinated efforts produce lasting results.

A contest, when run well, can produce results you can only image. Over half a million fans in less than a month? Write-ups in the New York Times and Mashable? Triple digit revenue increase? It's all possible with a successful contest or sweepstake.

Unique Targeted Content

Yet another tactic to market your Facebook Page is to use unique content only available on your Facebook Page to entice users to become fans. Just as Whitepapers and Free Guides help to increase conversions on your website, the same can be used on Facebook to convert fans.

As discussed in Section 2, content can be customized to be viewable by non-fans and fans to entice users to "Like" your Page. Utilize these areas to provide unique content, not found on your website or anywhere else on the web, only available to fans. Items such as videos, guides, blog posts, news, and coupons are all examples of unique targeted content that can be leveraged to promote your Facebook Page. Keep your target audience in mind and think about what you can offer. Execute the idea and continue to test its success. Vary up the content you offer, and don't forget to mention the unique content in cross platform messaging to entice more users to become fans.

"Like" Button and Privacy

In 2010, Facebook developed the "Like" button, a way for users to show their approval of content online and share it with friends. "Like" buttons can be placed on any webpage throughout the Internet. When a Facebook user presses the "Like" button, a link to the page is put on their wall and shared with their friends. In addition, your page will show in their "Likes and Interests" section and will allow you to publish updates to that particular user. You can even target advertising to those users who "Like" your content.

Depending on the "Like" button you implement on your website, you'll know exactly when a user clicks the button, and users will have the ability to comment in addition to "Like" the post which can make your link appear more prominent. To learn more about the Facebook "Like" button, and directions to placing it on your site go to the Social Plugins section of Facebook[19].

As you can imagine, adding the Facebook "Like" button to your site has the ability to promote your content to current fans, prospective fans, and friends of those fans. It's important to understand, however, the privacy implications involved in placing the button on your site.

Privacy Implications

Facebook's privacy policy is available online in its entirety, and contains information about privacy policies for Facebook Profiles, and all aspects of your interactions on Facebook. Facebook's "Like" button has caused a firestorm of controversy for many reasons. Users don't have to click the "Like" button for any of their information to be shared. The way the social plug-in works is Facebook collects the address of the website/page being visited and the Internet address of the visitor as soon as the page is loaded. Even if a user opts-out of sharing information, it can still be shared by friends to "partner sites" when they click the "Like" button. While businesses don't have access to this private profile information, Facebook does. Privacy advocates don't agree that this information should be provided, even to Facebook. It's important to understand exactly what information you're allowing Facebook to obtain from the users who visit your website and share your content.

Section 5
Measuring Results

Facebook Insights and Third Party Tools

There are many options on Facebook and on third party sites to monitor the results of your Facebook marketing. When proper goals are established at the beginning of your marketing campaign, measuring results becomes easier. In addition, benchmarks must be tracked to provide accurate results. Of course, benchmarks are easy to establish when you've never ventured down the path of Facebook marketing for your brand.

Each Administrator has access to Facebook Insights in the Administrator's Dashboard pictured below. Insights tracks data and activity on your Facebook Page including activity regarding your content and fans:

- Total "Likes" to establish growth trends of "Likes" over time
- Monthly active users and daily feedback to establish fan interaction over time
- Daily and monthly post views to monitor and track reach
- Daily and monthly un-"Likes" to monitor and track dissatisfaction
- Daily and monthly stream impressions to monitor and track reach
- Daily "Likes" and comments to monitor and track fan interaction per post over time
- Monthly gender and age data to monitor and track fan demographic trends
- Daily top referrers to your page to monitor and track how users find your Page

Using the information tracked above you can monitor the success of specific messaging and promotion efforts. Most of your stats are tracked over the entire lifetime of your Page, however some advanced stats are new to Facebook Insights and are only tracked for a short time. Insights is a free service and available to all Administrators of a particular Business Page. Simply click the Insights button on the Administrator's dashboard and you'll see a visual representation of many aspects of data tracked. In addition, Facebook offers the ability to export this data for easy conversion into charts, graphs, and reports.

Third party tools like Involvers Platform, Radian6, and Omniture will track more in-depth information and do the analysis work for you. They are paid platforms, and for large brands or agencies it's often worth the investment when you're involved with complex Facebook marketing efforts.

Google Analytics use to be yet another way to track success of your Facebook marketing. By adding Google Analytics code to a customized tab on your Facebook Page, you're able to monitor everything Google Analytics can monitor: conversion tracking, goal funnels, event tracking, page views and more. Recent changes, however, have restricted Google Analytics from working properly. Our hope is that with time developers will have solved this issue, as it can prove instrumental in determining the success or failure of your efforts.

The "Big Question": ROI

There's no one-size-fits-all answer for proving return on investment with your Facebook social media marketing. While goal conversions and sales are often the route taken to prove return on any marketing investment, it's important to understand in social media that it's about more. Social capital's worth is multifaceted. From reputation and brand recognition, to increased levels of trust and customer satisfaction, social media can provide your business with benefits that aren't easily quantifiable. That being said, there are still a few methods you can utilize to help you decide whether or not your investment in Facebook marketing is worth the investment spent in time and money.

Sales

Monitoring and measuring your sales before and after a particular social media marketing campaign can give some indication of levels of return, as well as cross domain tracking via Google Analytics to show goal conversions[20] (when Google Analytics and Facebook were working in tandem), polling, and Facebook Insights for applications which would enable fans to purchase directly on Facebook just to name a few.

It must be explained that not all factors will be taken into consideration with these methods. If your company suffers from seasonal ebbs and flows it can affect ROI calculations, in addition to unforeseen technical difficulties, reputation management issues, market changes, the list goes on and on. It's important to remember that the figures you obtain from tracking increases in sales will not be absolute, but analyzed over time can show patterns that allude to successes or failures.

Leads

Generating leads on Facebook Pages can be done directly, through implementation of customized applications and the analysis of data recorded through Facebook Insights and Google Analytics. Again, many factors should be taken into consideration including the effectiveness of calls to action which can affect results, and technical difficulties just to name a few.

Generating offsite leads can be tracked through Google Analytics with proper cross domain tracking, and goals and goal conversion funnels properly set up.

Reach

Mass media costs are often outside the financial budgets for many small businesses. With Facebook marketing businesses can reach a large audience at affordable prices. When comparing the cost of mass media and the cost to address a large audience on Facebook, the results can show that Facebook marketing can reduce financial costs while keeping similar effectiveness. The advantages that Facebook offers are metrics to track conversions that often television, print and radio cannot provide.

Product Development

A lot of time, money and effort can go into developing and testing new products. Using your Facebook Page as the venue for development and testing can often reduce these costs, and provide a savings that translates into return on the investment.

Customer Retention

Often, social media users utilize their personal profiles to praise or complain about a particular brand. It's hard to quantify the effect of these praises and complaints, but one way to measure your effectiveness in social media is to track brand mentions and sentiment. With tools like SocialMention.com you can take a baseline measurement of your sentiment and mentions before and after your Facebook marketing campaign.

Still not convinced? Find out how 77 companies used social media to successfully market their products, services, and brands in ways that were cost effective and worthwhile[21].

What is Success?

The success of your Facebook marketing campaign can be defined in many of the above mentioned ways: increases in sales, increases in lead generation, reach, product development and customer retention. In addition, social media marketing campaigns can help reduce customer service costs, increase the availability of product information and user materials to increase product satisfaction. The benefits are many. Establishing what you expect to get out of your efforts, and monitoring each of the ways your brand can be affected by a Facebook marketing campaign directly correlates to your own definition of success. You might even find that your Facebook marketing campaign establishes new metrics of success that you never thought of. Continuing to monitor all aspects of your campaign, putting the right tracking tools in place, and analyzing that data are the only ways you'll be able to truly figure out if your Facebook marketing campaign is a success.

Conclusion

Throughout this eBook we've discussed all aspects of Facebook, the history involved in the creation of this social media giant, how to develop the right Business Page for a brand, proper messaging techniques, ways to promote your Page and how to measure results. Now is the time to take the information we've provided and use it to build a successful Facebook marketing campaign that will effectively interact with your demographic on Facebook. Provide your brand with the online consumers it needs to flourish and grow in an ever changing market. It is our hope that you will be able to use the basic information provided and come up with your own creative, inventive, and interesting Facebook marketing opportunities applicable to your brand's overall goals.

Conclusion

BIBLIOGRAPHY/ RESOURCE LINKS

1   http://www.istrategylabs.com/2010/01/facebook-demographics-and-sta-
     tistics-report-2010-145-growth-in-1-year/

2   https://files.pbworks.com/download/vbcbn8hFkr/ddbworldwide-dropbox-
     aliciabrindak2/30907014/DDBOpinionwayFacebookenglishshortversion.pdf

3   http://www.youtube.com/watch?v=ofhwPC-5Ub4
4   http://searchnewscentral.com/20110117114/Technical/social-signals-and-
     search-engines.html
5   http://www.facebook.com/pages/create.php/terms.php#!/terms.php

6   http://www.hyperarts.com/blog/adding-iframe-application-to-facebook-
     fan-page/
7   http://www.forrester.com/empowered/tool_consumer.html

8   http://www.hubspot.com/marketing-webinar/science-of-facebook-market-
     ing-0/

9   http://www.hubspot.com/Portals/53/docs/science_of_facebook_zarrella_
     hubspot_webinar.pdf

10 http://www.hubspot.com/Portals/53/docs/science_of_facebook_zarrella_
     hubspot_webinar.pdf
11 http://go.vitrue.com/l/4162/2010-10-19/26PB9
12 http://www.insidefacebook.com/2011/02/27/like-button-full-story/
13 http://www.facebook.com/adsmarketing/
14 http://www.facebook.com/adsmarketing/index.php?sk=gettingstarted_
     audience
15 http://www.facebook.com/ad_guidelines.php
16 http://www.facebook.com/adsmarketing/index.php?sk=success
17 http://developers.facebook.com/policy/
18 http://www.facebook.com/promotions_guidelines.php
19 http://developers.facebook.com/docs/reference/plugins/like
20 http://code.google.com/apis/analytics/docs/tracking/gaTrackingSite.html
21 http://barnraisersllc.com/?p=2504

The Vertical Measures How-To Guide Series
Available Now!

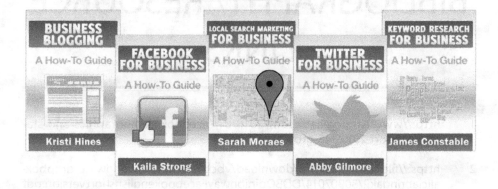

The Vertical Measures How-To Guide Series is for marketers, entrepreneur and executives that are ready to embrace emerging technologies that are taking businesses to the next level. The books highlight tactics that are worth focusing time and effort towards as well as those pointing out pitfalls to avoid.

The series provides deep insights into the world of emerging business technologies and covers topics including; Keyword Research, Facebook, Twitter, Local Search Marketing, Blogging and more.

- Succinct tactics for companies who are either using or plan to use new technologies to grow their business

- Written by industry experts with hands on experience in the field or discipline described

- Written specifically with the business and/or marketing user in mind – combining solid technical expertise with savvy advice.

Get discounted prices and take advantage of the opportunity to receive additional bonus materials for this series and other VM Press books like online at:
www.verticalmeasures.com/store/books